DEVON
Farmhouse
RECIPES

- *An Introduction* -

This wonderful collection of recipes is based on over fifty years of farmhouse cooking. It covers all the seasons and is an ideal way to begin using locally-sourced ingredients that will remind you of Devon.

Today there is a rich variety of ingredients all produced locally; while meat, vegetables, milk and cream have always been available, the rise of artisan produces has seen this range increase hugely in the last few years. Local now includes cheese, chocolate, flour, biscuits, salad leaves, herbs, gin and tea - all kinds of food and drink to make our life so much more exciting!

As always, cooking should be satisfying and fun; these recipes will help you have both in abundance. Enjoy!

Tamar Swift

- *Contents* -

EASY EATS

Beef Cobbler 6
Carrot & Tomato Soup 7
Crispy Chicken with Sage & Onion 8
Easy Pizza 10
Mrs W's Quick Fruit Cake 10

DINNER

Beef Casserole 12
Chicken Rissotto 13
Fish Pie 14
Meat Balls & Tomato Rice 16
Sausage & Ham Plait 16
Sage & Onion Toad in the Hole 17
Thyme & Leek Shepherd's Pie 18

VEG ON THE SIDE

Potato Pie 20
Stuffed Tomatoes 21
Winter Mashed Vegetables 22

PUDDINGS

Autumn Apple Tart 24
Treacle Tart 24
Bakewell Tart 25
Christmas Pudding 26
Strawberry Cake 27
Summer Pudding 28
Golden Apple Pudding 30

CHUTNEY, JAM, JELLY & MARMALADE

A *Devon Farmhouse* Chutney 32
Red Tomato & Marrow Chutney 33
Piccalilli 34
Gooseberry Jam 36
Raspberry Jam 36
Plum Jam 36
Redcurrant & Raspberry Jelly 37
Seville Orange Marmalade 38
Three Fruit Marmalade 38

CAKES & BAKES

Salted Caramel Shorties 40
Fruity Flapjacks 41
Chocolate Oatcakes 41
Chocolate Crumbles 42
Golden Syrup Gingerbread 42
Lemon Cake 44

CIDER & WINE

Apple Cider 46
Sloe Wine 46
Plum Wine 48
Redcurrant Wine 48

EASY

EATS

- *Beef Cobbler* -

For the beef...

1 yellow pepper or ⅓ jar mixed pepper anti pasta

1 red onion - *lightly chopped*

400g minced beef

1 tbsp dried rosemary - *chopped*

150ml gravy - *fresh or from granules*

For the 'cobbles'...

75g butter

200g flour

mixed herbs

1 egg

20g grated cheese

Carefully chop the pepper, mix well with the onion before frying until both begin to soften. If you use anti pasta, you will not need to add oil as the peppers will be naturally coated; if using a fresh pepper, use a little oil for frying. Add the meet and brown carefully, stirring to break up the mince. Stir in the rosemary, season to taste and add the gravy. Stir well and leave to simmer on a low heat for 40 minutes.

Meanwhile, make the 'cobbles' by rubbing the butter into the flour and mixed herbs. Beat the egg and add slowly until you have a stiff dough. If you like your cobbles to look neat and even, roll the dough out to approximately 2cm in depth and cut into 6 squares or rounds. If you prefer a more informal look, hand press the dough out, divide into 6 pieces and flatten further to a depth of your choice.

Place the minced beef mixture in an oven-proof dish, add the cobbles on the top, sprinkle with the grated cheese (something robust like a good blue cheese) and bake in the oven for 15-20 minutes at 350°F/180°C until golden brown and bubbling.

- *Carrot & Tomato Soup* -

1 small onion or leak - *chopped*

150g carrots - *roughly chopped*

400g tin chopped tomatoes

cheddar cheese for serving

Gently fry the chopped onion in a pan until translucent. Add the carrots, tomatoes, stock and sugar and stir well. Season to taste.

Simmer for around 45 minutes or until the carrots are tender. Blend in a liquidiser; check the seasoning before serving.

A sprinkling of grated Davidstow Cheddar and a fresh loaf of bread is really all this needs to make it the perfect lunch on a cold day.

- *Crispy Chicken with Sage & Onion* -

This is the easiest chicken dish in the world, and yet looks and tastes as though you've spent hours preparing it.

4 chicken breasts

a little plain flour

1 egg - *beaten*

120g sage & onion packet stuffing*

2 cloves garlic

1 bunch parsley *(optional)*

Slice the chicken in half lengthways and flatten each piece with a rolling pin to make into thin escalopes. In a shallow dish, mix the stuffing with the crushed garlic and if using, fresh parsley. Roll the chicken in the flour, dip in the beaten egg and finally give it a good coating of the stuffing mixture.

Place each one on a lightly oiled baking tray and cook for 30 minutes at 375°F/180°C or until cooked through. *Remember: chicken must be fully cooked before eating. If you find the stuffing is beautifully brown but the chicken isn't quite cooked, cover with foil and return to the oven until cooked through.*

Serve with a speedy salad – either home or shop-assembled.

*Packet stuffing comes in various flavours; choose one to suit your taste and don't be put off by any thoughts of them being old-fashioned. While you could make your own stuffing, by the time you've done that, you could have this whole recipe in the oven cooking.

- Easy Pizza -

The base is made like a scone dough, which makes thus both quick and easy.

175g self raising flour

50g butter

110g cheese

1 egg

2 tbsp milk

1 small onion

200g chopped tomatoes - *tinned or fresh*

16g tin sweetcorn

2 rashers bacon

2 mushrooms

pinch mixed herbs

Rub the butter into the flour, add the milk and egg and half of the cheese if you want a cheesy base.

Roll out the dough and place into a greased 20cm Victoria sandwich tin. Add the toppings and sprinkle with the cheese. Cook for about 30 minutes in a moderate oven (350°F/180°C).

- Mrs W's Quick Fruit Cake -

110g butter

225g demerara sugar

250g mixed fruit

175g self raising flour

240ml milk

1 tsp mixed spice

2 tsp baking powder

3 large eggs

add a small apple, if liked

Into a large saucepan put the butter, sugar, fruit, milk and apple, if using. Heat over a gentle heat until boiling. Cool – for about 20 minutes.

Sieve in the flour, spice and baking powder, add the beaten eggs and mix well. Put into greased 15cm cake tin.

Cook for 30 minutes at 150°C/300°F. Leave in the tin to cool completely before removing.

DINNER

- *Beef Casserole* -

For the casserole...

1 onion - *chopped*

450g stewing beef - *cut into cubes*

200g of preferred vegetables*

570ml stock

1tbsp gravy thickening

For the dumplings...

125g self raising flour

50g butter

pinch salt

1 tsp baking powder

water - *to make a dough*

Chop and fry the onion in a little oil and set aside. Brown the beef, before mixing with the onions in a casserole dish. *Add any vegetables that you like; a good selection might be: chopped carrots, swede, mushrooms, tomatoes.* Add enough stock to comfortably cover all the vegetables.

Bring the casserole to the boil before cooking at 325°F/170°C for 2-3 hours. Before serving thicken with gravy thickening.

Potatoes can be added to the vegetables, but I prefer to cook these separately.

For the dumplings:

In a bowl, sift the flour, salt and baking powder. Add the butter and mix with cold water. Once thoroughly mixed, roll into balls.

Add the dumplings to the casserole after it has thickened and cook for a further 20 minutes.

- *Chicken Risotto* -

This dinner recipe is very quick and easy - all the ingredients go in at once and it's brilliant for using up any of those leftovers!

1 onion - *chopped*

400g chicken or mushroom soup diluted with 120ml water

175g long grain rice

mushrooms, sweetcorn or any vegetable you like

225g chicken or turkey - *this can be fresh or taken from a cooked bird or leftovers (shredded)*

salt & pepper - *to taste*

Fry the onion and cook in a pan with a little oil. Add the chicken soup, water, mushrooms or your choice of veg, stir well. Cook the rice, drain and rinse with boiling water.

Mix everything together and turn into a greased dish. Top with grated cheese and brown either in the oven or under a hot grill.

Excellent served with peas and crusty bread.

- *Fish Pie* -

Choosing a variety of fish for this homely recipe works so well. It will add a lovely range of textures and colour - especially when using cooked salmon.

600g fish fillet
(mixed - salmon, cod, haddock)

nutmeg

900g mashed potato

sprigs of parsley - *chopped*

milk

100g clotted cream

Remove all the skin and bones from the fish, flake up with a fork and put into a greased pie dish. Cover with clotted cream. Sprinkle with chopped parsley and soften with a little milk.

Spread the mashed potatoes evenly over the fish, fork up and dot with small flecks of butter. Decorate with a few gratings of nutmeg and bake in a moderate oven (350°F/180°C) for about 30 minutes or until golden brown.

Serve with bread and beans or peas & parsley sauce, which compliment the pie very nicely.

- *Meat Balls & Tomato Rice* -

225g minced beef

40g fresh breadcrumbs

1 egg - *to bind*

2 tsp fruit chutney

110g long grain rice

300g condensed tomato soup

275ml water

mixed dried herbs

butter or oil - *for frying*

Mix together the meat, breadcrumbs, chutney and seasoning before binding with the beaten egg. Using your hands, form the mixture into balls, roll in a little flour and fry until brown.

Put the rice into a greased casserole dish and place the meat balls on top. Heat the soup, water and herbs before pouring over the meatballs and rice. If necessary, add a little more water to make sure all the rice is covered.

Cover and bake for 45 mins - 1 hour at 325°F/170°C.

- *Sausage & Ham Plait* -

This is an ideal recipe to take on picnics, or to cut up for lunch boxes.
It is also delicious with salads and it freezes beautifully.

225g ready-rolled shortcrust pastry or home-made, made with 225g self raising flour and 110g butter

175g cooked chopped ham

225g pork sausage meat

2-3 spring onions

1 tsp mustard

1-2 tbsp chopped fresh parsley

2 hard boiled eggs - *sliced*

1 beaten egg - *for glazing*

Open or roll out the pastry to a 25cm square. Mix together the ham, sausage meat, onions, mustard and parsley. Place half the mixture down the centre of the pastry leaving equal sides of empty pastry.

Then place the sliced eggs on top and cover with the rest of the mixture. Brush the pastry with the beaten egg. Now cut the pastry sides at 45° angles sloping downwards in 1cm strips (rather like a fish fin). Lift alternate strips over the filling to form a roll resembling a plait. Brush with beaten egg. Place on a baking tray on the top shelf of the oven and cook for 10 minutes at 400°F/200°C. Then reduce heat to 350°F/180°C for a further 35 minutes, or until sausage meat is cooked. Serve with crusty bread and peas and enjoy hot or cold.

- Sage & Onion Toad in the Hole -

450g sausages

3 tbsp vegetable oil

110g plain flour

pinch salt

275ml milk

1 small onion - *chopped*

3 or 4 sage leaves - *chopped finely*

1 egg

milk

Place sausages in an oven proof dish with 3 tbsp of vegtable oil and cook for 15 minutes.

Mix the flour and salt in a bowl, stir in the onion, sage, egg & milk. Beat until smooth and pour over the sausages and return to the oven.

Cook until golden brown and well risen at 375°F/190°C for approximately 40 minutes.

- *Thyme & Leek Shepherd's Pie* -

Always a favourite and so easy to make.

800g potatoes

3 tbsp milk

25g butter

salt & pepper

oil - *for frying*

1 large onion - *chopped*

450g minced lamb or minced beef

150ml stock

1 tbsp Worcester sauce

2 tomatoes - *chopped*

Cook floury potatoes until soft and mash with the milk, butter, salt & pepper. Heat a little oil in a frying pan and fry one large chopped onion. Add the minced lamb *(this is a traditional recipe but instead you can use minced beef)* and cook for a further 5-6 minutes.

Stir in the stock, Worcester sauce, tomatoes, salt & pepper and add any herbs, if liked.

Simmer for 5 minutes. Spoon into an ovenproof dish, cover with the mashed potato, making sure you spread to the edges. Fluff up the surface with a fork, then dot with butter.

Bake for 35-40 minutes at 350°F/180°C or until golden brown. Serve with fresh vegetables.

VEG
ON THE SIDE

- *Potato Pie* -

This delicious potato pie serves **4.**

900g potatoes

1 level tsp dry mustard
(optional)

1 small onion - *chopped*

salt & pepper

For the filling...

4 eggs

225g grated cheese

570ml milk

25g butter

salt & pepper

Grease a 1.7l ovenproof dish. Boil the potatoes and mash well before adding the mustard, onion, salt & pepper. Line the base and sides of the dish, forking it up well round the sides.

Break the eggs into a basin and beat well before adding the cheese, milk and seasoning.

Pour into the potato case. Spread the top with dabs of butter. Bake in a moderate oven (350°F/180°C) for 1 hour.

- Stuffed Tomatoes -

Add some colour to your plate and try this recipe using Heirloom tomatoes - known for their gorgeous rainbow colours and sweet, juicy flavour.

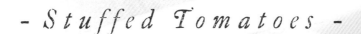

6 large Heirloom tomatoes

100g mushrooms - *finely chopped*

50g leek - *finely chopped*

50g yellow pepper - *finely chopped*

40g grated cheese

75g fresh breadcrumbs

1 egg - *beaten*

salt & pepper

Cut the tops from the tomatoes and remove the centre with a teaspoon.

Lightly fry the mushrooms and leeks until soft. Add the peppers and stir well. Add the cheese, breadcrumbs, tomato pulp and beaten egg and combine. Season to taste. Fill the tomatoes and replace the tops.

Place the filled tomatoes on a baking tray lined with greaseproof paper and cook in a moderate oven (350°F-180°C) for approximately 30 minutes. Serve on buttered toast, or with a main dish of your choice.

- *Winter Mashed Vegetables* -

Very good served with Christmas dinner.

350g parsnips

350g swede

70ml sour cream

I level tbsp hot horseradish

2 tsp thyme leaves

salt & pepper

butter - *for frying*

I small onion - *chopped*

50g fresh white breadcrumbs

25g grated parmesan cheese

Peel the parsnips and the swede, then chop and rinse. Boil together in salted water until tender. Drain well and mash until smooth, leaving a little texture. Stir in the cream, horseradish and half the thyme. Season well with salt and pepper.

Spoon into a buttered, shallow ovenproof dish and set aside. Melt a little butter in a frying pan and fry the onion for 5-6 minutes or until it's looking golden.

Mix in the breadcrumbs and stir over the heat to brown and crisp a little. Season and add the other half of the thyme. Scatter over the mashed vegetables and sprinkle parmesan over the top.

This dish may be kept covered in the fridge at this point for up to a day or frozen for up to a month. Bake at 375°F/190°C for 25-30 minutes if just made or 35-40 minutes if chilled, until brown and crispy on the top.

PUDDINGS

- *Autumn Apple Tart* -

We all enjoy a traditional mincemeat tart at Christmas, however this recipe is great for those of you who like a slightly less sweet dish.

For the pastry...

110g plain flour

50g butter

1 egg - *beaten*

For the filling...

1 cooking apple - *cored, peeled & sliced*

150g mincemeat

Make the pastry by rubbing the butter into the flour until it resembles breadcrumnbs. Add enough egg to bring the pastry together and chill for 20 minutes. Divide the pastry into two and roll out each half to the same size as the tin.

To help balance the sweetness, line your tin with pastry as usual, then spread with a thin layer of mincemeat and cover this with a layer of sliced cooking apple.

Top with a further layer of pastry and bake in a moderate oven (375°F/190°C) for approximately 30 minutes.

- *Treacle Tart* -

225g shortcrust pastry

110g fresh white breadcrumbs

1 large cooking apple

4 tbsp golden syrup

Line a 20cm flan dish with the pastry. Peel, core and slice the apple and place on the pastry.

Mix the syrup and breadcrumbs and pour over the apple. Decorate with pastry trimmings in a lattice pattern.

Bake for 45 minutes at 400°F/200°C until golden.

- Bakewell Tart -

To make this popular tart even more delicious, add flaked almonds and whole raspberries on top of the mixture before placing it in the oven to bake.

For the pastry...

110g plain flour

50g butter

1 egg - *beaten*

For the filling...

50g butter

50g sugar

50g semolina

1 egg - *beaten*

1 tsp almond essence

½ tsp baking powder

2 tbsp apricot jam

Make up the pastry, as for Autumn Apple Tart, and line a deep greased sandwich tin. Spread the jam over the pastry.

Melt the butter and sugar in a saucepan and stir in the semolina, cook for a few minutes stirring all the time.

Remove from the heat, cool a little and add the almond essence, stirring well. Mix together the baking powder before adding to the almond mixture. Add the beaten egg and the baking powder.

Pour the filling over the jam, spreading evenly. Bake in a moderate oven (350°F/180°C) for 25-30 minutes.

- *Christmas Pudding* -

What would Christmas be without the pud!

50g almonds - *chopped*

2 medium apples - *grated, no need to peel*

1 good sized carrot - *grated*

1 orange - *grated and juiced*

1 lemon - *grated and juiced*

225g suet/vegetarian alternative

3 eggs

336g demerara sugar

175g self raising flour

225g sultanas

112g raisins

225g currants

50g cherries - *chopped*

50g dates - *chopped*

50g peel - *chopped*

400g white breadcrumbs

½ tsp mixed spice

½ tsp cinnamon

¼ tsp ground ginger

custard or clotted cream for serving

Mix all the ingredients together in a large bowl and allow to stand overnight. The next day, give the mixture another good mix *and don't forget to make your wish.* Then comfortably fill the well greased basins.

Cover with several layers of greaseproof paper (and pudding cloths if you wish) and gently cook for 5 - 6 hours.

When required for use, cook for a further 1½ hours. Serve with a sprinkling of caster sugar, custard or clotted cream.

- *Strawberry Cake* -

Here is a very easy recipe and one of the tastiest ways to serve strawberries.

For the sponge...

3 eggs

75g caster sugar

1 tbsp hot water

75g plain flour

For the cake mixture...

450g strawberries

2 tbsp caster sugar

300ml carton of double cream

Make a whisked sponge by mixing together the eggs, caster sugar and hot water, before folding in the plain flour.

With a little butter, grease and line a swiss roll tin. Pour in the sponge mixture and tap the tin gently to even it out. Bake in a hot oven (375°F/190°C) for approximately 12-15 minutes.

Turn out and allow to cool. *This can be made beforehand and frozen.*

Sprinkle the caster sugar over the strawberries and leave in the fridge until needed. Take a 300ml carton of double cream and whip gently until it holds its shape. Cut the cake in half (cross-wise) spread one half with cream, then scatter the strawberries over. Place the other half of the sponge on top, then add the cream and the rest of the strawberries.

Place in the fridge for 1-2 hours to settle before serving.

- *Summer Pudding* -

Choose a variety of fruit, the more you have, the more interesting the pudding.

900g summer fruits - *strawberries, raspberries, gooseberries, blueberries. red & black currants, rhubarb, blackberries or any available fruits*

110g sugar

8 slices of white bread - *crusts removed*

cream for serving

Cook your choice of fruit in a saucepan with the sugar and a little water until softened but not broken up. Line a 1.2l pudding basin with slices of white bread, cutting a round for the bottom.

Fill the lined basin with the fruit, top with bread and cover with a saucer or small plate with a weight on top.

Chill in the fridge for several hours. Turn out just before serving and spoon extra fruit over the top.

Serve with cream.

- *Golden Apple Pudding* -

This dish is a change from all the sweet things around Christmas.

For the pudding...

110g self raising flour

50g suet/vegetarian alternative

pinch salt

cold water to mix

For the filling...

100g golden syrup

1 medium sized apple -
chopped finely

custard or cream for serving

Grease a 450ml basin.

Mix together the self raising flour, suet and the pinch of salt in a bowl, then add enough cold water to make a soft dough. Divide the dough into two and place one half in the bottom of the basin. Cover with 50g of golden syrup.

Put the apple on top of the mixture, then add the 50g of remaining golden syrup and finally top with the rest of the dough.

Cover with greased foil and place in a saucepan with a lid. Add enough water to sit half-way up the bowl and bring to the boil. Simmer for 1 ½ hours. Do not allow to boil dry.

Serve with lashings of custard.

CHUTNEY, JAM, JELLY & MARMALADE

- *A Devon Farmhouse Chutney* -

This chutney is so easy to make, stores well and really improves with keeping.

900g tomatoes - *ripe and green*

900g apples

450g sultanas

450g onions

5g red chillies

725ml vinegar

900g dark brown sugar

50g salt

25g ground ginger

Grease the pan to make sure the mixture does not stick.

Mince together the tomatoes, the apples (no need to core or peel), the sultanas, onions and red chillies. Place the mixture into the greased pan.

Add the vinegar, dark brown sugar, salt and the ground ginger. Bring to a gentle boil, making sure you stir occasionally.

Cool slightly before potting.

- *Red Tomato & Marrow Chutney* -

A delicious chutney recipe that is a perfect addition to any curry dish.

450g marrow - *after peeling*

225g onions - *chopped*

50g tomatoes - *skinned & chopped*

225g sultanas

150g white sugar

175g brown sugar

275ml vinegar

1 tsp ground ginger

1 tbsp mixed pickling spice (tied in a piece of muslin)

1 tsp salt

Cut the marrow into small cubes and put into a large pan with the onions, tomatoes, sultanas, sugar, vinegar and spices.

Stir over low heat until the sugar is dissolved, then allow to simmer for approximately 1½ hours, stirring occasionally to prevent burning.

If you wish, gently mash the mixture while it cooks. You will know the chutney is cooked when you can draw the spoon through it and leave a trail that does not immediately fill with liquid.

Pot up into hot dry jars. Seal with vinegar proof lids when cold.

- *Piccalilli* -

Choose a selection of the following ingredients, or any other vegetables you prefer.
Vegetables should be washed and peeled and have a combined weight of 1.8kg.

cauliflower

runner beans

cucumber

onions

marrow

green tomatoes

salt

vinegar

10g turmeric

10g mustard

10g ground ginger

112g brown sugar

2 tbsp cornflour

chillies - *if liked*

Cut the vegetables into small pieces, spread on large plates, salt well, cover and leave to stand overnight. The next day, drain all the vegetables thoroughly.

To every 1.8kg of vegetables, you will need 150ml vinegar, 10g turmeric, 10g mustard, 10g ground ginger, chillies and 112g brown sugar.

Boil the ingredients together in a large pan, then add the vegetables and cook slowly for 30 minutes.

Mix 2 tbsp cornflour with a little of the liquid and add to the mixture stirring well all the time. Cook for a further 15 minutes or until vegetables are tender, consistently stirring to prevent burning.

Pot up while warm and seal with vinegar-proof lids when cold. Allow to mature for a few weeks before using.

- Gooseberry Jam -

1.4kg gooseberries

570ml water

1.4kg sugar

Top and tail the gooseberries and put them into a large pan. Bring them slowly to the boil and simmer for about 20 - 30 minutes until the skins are tender. Add the sugar and stir until dissolved before bringing it back to the boil for about 15 -20 minutes. *Test for a set and whilst still warm, pot up. Leave to cool before covering with waxed discs and lids. *To test for a set, simply pop 2 small plates in the freezer for 10 minutes. When your jam is ready, place a large drop on a plate. If the jam sets and wrinkles when moved with your finger, it's ready. If not, boil for a little longer and test again.

- Raspberry Jam -

Raspberries come into season in July. When they are readily available in shops, and 'pick your own' is available at some fruit farms. They really do make a lovely jam – and this recipe is so easy! You can always be sure of a good set.

900g raspberries

900g sugar

Cook the fruit slowly for 10-15 minutes in a saucepan. Add the sugar and stir until dissolved. Boil again for 10 minutes. Test for a set and pot up as before.

- Plum Jam -

675g plums - *after stones have been removed*

675g sugar

275ml water - *if plums are firm, or add less water if they are soft*

Cook the plums and water slowly, until soft. Add the sugar and stir over a low heat until dissolved, then boil rapidly until a little tried on a cold plate wrinkles when moved with your finger (approximately 15 minutes). Test for a set and pot up as before.

- *Redcurrant &*
Raspberry Jelly -

675g redcurrants

225g raspberries

855ml water

450g sugar to each 570ml juice

Wash the currants and raspberries, there is no need to remove the stalks. Put the washed currants and berries into a pan with water and simmer until soft for approximately 20-30 minutes, stirring and pressing the fruit against the side of the pan to extract as much juice as possible.

Pour into a jelly bag and allow to drip – if you squeeze the bag you will get more juice into the pan. Add the sugar and stir over a low heat until it dissolves, then increase heat and boil rapidly for approximately 15 minutes.

Test for a set and, as before, pour into really hot jars. Cover with waxed discs and lids when cold.

- *Seville Orange Marmalade* -

675g seville oranges

1 lemon

2.5l water

1.5kg sugar

1.75l cold water

---

*For Three Fruit
Marmalade...*

1 grapefruit

1 lemon

4 seville oranges
(approximately 675g in
combined weight)

1.75l water

1.5kg sugar

*Use the same method as for
Seville Orange Marmalade*

Wash the oranges, peel and remove all the pith and pips (tie these in a muslin bag). Cut the peel into thin shreds and, in a large bowl, combine with the fruit, juice, and bag of pith and pips.

Add 1.75l cold water, cover and leave to stand overnight. The next day, turn the contents into a large pan and bring to the boil, simmering gently for approximately 2 hours and 15 minutes until the peel is soft and until the liquid has reduced greatly.

Remove the bag of pips and squeeze as much liquid as you can from it. Stir in the sugar and when dissolved, bring back to a fast boil, boiling rapidly for approximately 15-20 minutes or until the ingredients set when tested on a cold plate. Stand for 10 minutes before potting. Leave until completely cold before covering with waxed discs and lids.

CAKES & BAKES

- Salted Caramel Shorties -

These are a real afternoon treat and are very quick to make.

For the caramel...

75g light brown caster sugar

15g salt flakes

For the shortbread...

110g butter

125g plain flour

75g soft brown sugar

For the topping...

200g salted caramel chocolate

NOTE: *Care must be taken when heating sugar as it boils at a far higher temperature (around 325°F/160°C) than water (250°F/100°C) and can spit.*

Line two baking trays with baking parchment or use the same one twice.

Gently heat the sugar until melted in a heavy-based saucepan, stirring frequently and making sure it doesn't 'catch' and burn. Continue heating gently until the sugar takes on a dark, glossy colour and texture. At this point, remove it from the heat, add the salt flakes and give a final stir. Now pour this sugar and salt mixture onto the lined baking tray, tilt to make sure it reaches all the corners and leave it to set. Once completely cold, break the caramel into small pieces and set aside.

Now for the shortbread: sift the flour and sugar together into a bowl and rub in the butter. Gently knead in the caramel pieces until they are evenly distributed. Turn the caramel dough onto a floured board and divide into 18 pieces. Roll each piece into a ball, place them onto a tray lined with baking parchment and flatten slightly. Bake for 15 minutes in a moderate oven (350°F/1980°C) and leave to cool.

Melt the caramel chocolate in a bowl over a pan of barely simmering water. When melted, either add a teaspoon full to each of the shorties or drizzle the chocolate over each one. The toppping should harden quickly so you can eat them very soon!

- Chocolate Oatcakes -

225g butter

175g dark soft brown sugar

25g cocoa powder

225g porridge oats

225g plain dark chocolate

Grease a square 18cm shallow cake tin. Melt the butter in saucepan over a low heat. Remove the pan from the heat and add the sugar, cocoa and oats.

Stir the mixture well to combine all the ingredients, before placing it into the cake baking tin. Bake for approximately 15 minutes or until it's bubbling.

Allow the oatcake to cool. Melt the plain chocolate gently in a bowl over a saucepan of hot water, then pour it on top of the cooled oatcake, spreading it flat with a palette knife.

Leave in a cool place until the chocolate is set, then cut into squares and enjoy!

- Fruity Flapjacks -

175g porridge oats

25g soft brown sugar

85g soft butter

2 tbsp syrup

75g dried fruit - *raisins, sultanas, currants*

2 tbsp black treacle

8 glace cherries - *cut into quarters*

1 apple - *thinly sliced*

Put the butter, sugar, syrup and black treacle in a pan and heat gently until melted. Add the oats, fruit and cherries, stirring well until everything is coated. Put half of the mixture into a greased tin and press down firmly and evenly.

Place a layer of sliced apple on top and add the rest of the mixture to cover the apple, forming a kind of flapjack sandwich. Cook for 20-30 minutes at 375°F/190°C.

Cut into fingers and remove from the tin when completely cold.

- Chocolate Crumbles -

A really straightforward and quick non-cook teatime treat.
This is one of those recipes children could easily be asked to make.

100g butter

2 tbsp golden syrup

25g caster sugar

4 tsp drinking chocolate or cocoa powder

250g digestive biscuits

Melt the butter, golden syrup, sugar and cocoa powder in a saucepan. Keeping the biscuits in their unopened packaging, gently crush them with a rolling pin. Now cut off one end and pour the crushed biscuits into the golden syrup mixture and stir well.

Don't worry about uneven crushing – this will simply add greater texture to the *Crumbles*. Spread your lovely mixture into a shallow 18cm square tin and leave in the fridge to harden.

When set, cut into squares and serve with a cup of tea and a magazine or game.

- Golden Syrup Gingerbread -

This is best cooked in a square cake tin as it's easier to cut up. It does rise considerably, so you will need a large tin.

100g butter

100g sugar

75g black treacle

100g golden syrup

150ml milk

1 egg - *beaten*

200g plain flour

3-4 tsp ground ginger

1 tsp bicarbonate soda

clotted cream - *for serving*

Melt the butter, sugar, treacle, syrup and milk over a low heat. Cool until lukewarm. Add the sieved dry ingredients and egg. Beat well until smooth.

Pour into the tin and bake at 300°F/150°C until it springs back when pressed gently, approximately 1½ hours.

This cake is so good for freezing. I usually make the whole amount, cut the cake in half when cold and freeze half. It is also useful for emergencies as it defrosts very quickly and is great if warmed and served with Devon clotted cream.

- *Lemon Cake* -

A wonderfully effortless cake to make that bursts with zesty lemon flavour.

110g butter

175g caster sugar

2 eggs - *beaten*

milk

175g self raising flour

50g granulated sugar

grated rind and juice of
2 lemons

Grease and line a 900g loaf tin.

Cream the butter, caster sugar and lemon rind until fluffy. Beat in the eggs slowly - don't worry if the mixture curdles. Mix together the flour with 4 tbsp milk to make a soft paste, before adding this to the butter mixture and stirring well. Place everything in the loaf tin and smooth the top.

Bake in a moderate oven (350°F / 180°C) for 45-50 minutes or until firm and golden, and shrinking from the sides of the tin. Prepare the lemon syrup by heating the lemon juice and granulated sugar gently until the sugar dissolves.

As soon as the cake is out of the oven, and while it's still in the tin, prick it all over with a skewer and pour over the syrup. Leave the cake in the tin until cold.

Tasty tip: try using other citrus fruits such as limes or oranges - they work just as well!

CIDER & WINE

- *Apple Cider* -

Take note: be very steady on opening the bottles as this cider can be really 'lively' – best opened carefully in the sink.

1.35kg cooking apples

900g sugar

2 large lemons

6.8l cold water

Check the apples are free from any maggots, then cut them in pieces with the core and peel. Blast them for a few seconds in the liquidiser (just enough to break them up). My original recipe tells me to put them through a mincer, but a food processor is much easier.

Put the apples into a pan and pour over 6.8l of cold water. Stir well, cover and leave for a week stirring every day. At the end of the week, strain, then add the sugar and grated rind and juice of the lemons. Leave for 24 hours then strain again and bottle into glass (not plastic) screw top bottles.

The cider will be ready in a week, but is better if left for 2-3 weeks.

- *Sloe Wine* -

This is one of my favourite recipes; sloes are still found on the moors but you may have to look carefully to find then.

4.5l sloes

4.5l boiling water

1.35kg sugar

10g yeast

Pour the boiling water over the sloes, cover and leave to stand for four days stirring each day. Strain.

Add the yeast and sugar and leave for another four days, again stirring each day. Put into a demijohn, insert an air lock and leave to work. Rack off after it has cleared.

Cork the demijohn and leave for approximately 3 months before bottling.

- Plum Wine -

1.8kg plums

5g root ginger

4 cloves

1 lemon - *sliced*

4.5l water

1.35kg sugar

25g Baker's yeast

Cut up the plums and remove the stones. Bruise the ginger and add to the plums with the cloves and sliced lemon. Cover with the boiling water and stir well. Cover and leave for four days, stirring each day with a wooden or plastic spoon.

Strain through muslin onto the sugar, warming a little of the mixture first to help the yeast work.

Lastly, mix the yeast with a little of the liquid before adding it to the wine. Leave everything in the pan overnight and the next day transfer to a fermentation jar to work. When it has ceased working, cork the jar and leave for several months before bottling. Best left a year before drinking.

- Redcurrant Wine -

1.8kg redcurrants

1.5kg sugar

4.5l boiling water

25g bakers yeast

Pour the boiling water over the currants and when luke warm, mash well with a wooden spoon. Cover and leave for four days stirring daily. Then strain well through muslin. Heat approximately 570ml of the juice in a saucepan, then pour this back into the pan. This is just to take the chill off the wine before adding the yeast.

In the meantime, mix the yeast with a little of the liquid then add it to the wine together with the sugar. Stir well and allow to stand overnight. The next day transfer to a fermentation jar, insert an air lock and leave to work. When you think it has stopped working, rack off and leave again to clear.

You can bottle approximately 6 months later after which it is best left for 12 months before drinking.